One Man's Dream

The World-Wide Swap And Trade/The Gift Challenge

By: Laura Baillum

Published by Bookmarketeers.com

Cover Design: Bookmarketeers.com

Editing Support: Bookmarketeers.com

Printed in the United States of America

Inspirational Disclaimer

This book is dedicated to the memory of dreams and to the unshakable belief that one family's vision can ignite hope, courage, and creativity in the world. Every page you hold is rooted in the spirit of truth, love, and legacy crafted to remind us that when one dreamer dares to believe, the ripple of that belief can move mountains.

Any resemblance to actual events or people is intentional in spirit, yet adapted through the lens of creative storytelling because stories live not only in facts, but in faith.

From one dreamer to the world: when one family dares to believe, the whole world gains permission to dream.

DEDICATION

To my loving husband, **Leandrew**— you are my heart, my friend, my forever.

A love like ours will never end, and this book is living proof. It exists because of you—because you believed, because you dreamed, because you never gave up. When hope seemed distant, when dreams felt far, you stood steady and reminded me of what was possible. You always said, *"We can,"* and in your voice I found my courage.

You lifted my hopes, you steadied my way, turning every night into a brighter day.

With your gentle strength, you showed me that everything fantastic begins not with ***me***, but with ***we.***

Leandrew, your faith has been my guiding light. You gave me the courage to write, to fight, to believe in something greater than myself. This book was written for you, about you, and because of you. Without your dream, *One Man's Dream* would not exist. It carries your vision, your spirit, your heart on every page.

So here I stand, with love so deep, a vow I promise forever to keep.

For every dream—both old and new—

I dedicate them all to my love, Leandrew.

YOU

This story is ours. It was born from my heart but inspired by your brilliance. You are my living inspiration, my endless encouragement, and the reason this book will reach the world.

Always and forever, With all my love, **Laura Baillum**

ACKNOWLEDGMENTS

To **Leandrew, my loving husband**, thank you for never giving up on your dream and for trusting me to walk beside you as we brought your vision into the world. The day we sat together and pieced your prototype game board was the very moment *One Man's Dream* truly came alive. I remember watching the light in your eyes, the joy on your face as you touched and held something that had once only lived in your imagination. At that moment, I knew what I had to do—I had to share your brilliance with the world. That was the day I began writing, and that was the day *One Man's Dream* was born. This book is not just a story; it is your legacy, our legacy, and a testimony of faith, determination, and love.

To our **entire family**—your unwavering love and support made this real. Every idea shared, every word of encouragement, every moment of belief carried us through. I could not have done this without you.

To my beautiful mother, **Francine**, I love you with all that I am. Thank you for giving me life, for nurturing me with strength and wisdom, and for always being my guiding light.

To my siblings—**Juanita, Robert, and Tina**—may God continue to bless you and keep you safe. Thank you for always being there. And to my sister **Juanita**, I have to say it again: *thank you, thank you, thank you!* You have always had my back, no matter what the circumstances. I love you endlessly for that.

To my children—**Diane, Antoinette, Brenda, and Rodney Jr.**—I love you more than words can express. Continue to grow, to push forward, and to never stop learning. I am so very proud of each of you and the incredible people you have become.

To my grandchildren—**Shameer, Rodney, Ah'laysia, and Amorah**—Mommom loves you with all her heart. I look forward with joy to seeing all the amazing things life has in store for you.

And remember what Mommom has always told you: *"Educate yourself on purpose."* Never forget that wisdom will guide you through everything.

And finally, to all my **family and friends**—I love you always. Each of you are a piece of my story, and your love has fueled my spirit. Thank you for being part of this journey.

THE CONVERSATION

The kitchen smelled like cinnamon toast and fresh coffee—Laura's way of saying, *I'm listening*. Lee sat at the table, notebook open, his voice pulsing with excitement as he flipped through pages filled with sketches and scribbles. Laura, robe tied, cup in hand, leaned in with patient curiosity.

"You remember how Monopoly brings people together?" Lee began. "This is like that—but next level. Players aren't just playing to win fake money. They're building connections, sharing real gifts, and completing trades from city to city."

Laura sipped her coffee and nodded. "Okay, slow down. Walk me through this, one step at a time."

Lee grinned, grateful for her grounded energy. "Alright. Each player starts with 5,000 digital coins—customized with their name or avatar. They choose a city to begin in—say, Philadelphia. Their mission is to collect 1,000 unique coins from other players in that city. That makes one *lot*."

Laura tilted her head. "So, ten lots equals a state?"

"Exactly. And when you complete all 50 states—bam! You're in the annual Gift Challenge finale. That's the big moment. We're talking about life-changing prizes, media attention, and global participation. But the real beauty is in the process—how people connect along the way." Laura looked impressed. "And these coins—are they just tokens?"

"No, that's the best part. They represent real gifts—either digital or physical. You can trade a coin, but to earn it, you must swap a token to collect cities that will then equal state values. It could be a handwritten note, a book, a video message—something with personal meaning." Laura smiled, seeing the heart of it now. "So, it's a game built on generosity."

"Exactly. Strategy meets story. Competition meets connection. It's called *The World-Wide Swap and Trade / The Gift Challenge* because it's more than a game—it's a global movement of giving."

Laura tapped the notebook. "We'll need rules, designs, digital safety, platforms... And if you want this to work across age groups, the interface has to be simple and engaging."

Lee nodded. "That's where I need you." "You always need me," she teased.

"I *always* need you," he said sincerely. They both laughed.

Laura stood, reached into the cabinet, and pulled out a clean notepad. "Then let's build it right. What's first? Platform? Target audience? Branding?"

Lee looked at her like she was magic.

"We start with the blueprint," he said. "Then we bring the family in." Laura flipped open her notepad. "Let's make this dream a reality."

And so, over coffee and cinnamon toast, The World-Wide Swap and Trade / The Gift Challenge took its first steps from idea… to plan.

PREFACE

Most of my years, I have been extremely happy, loved and in love. But as with all of us, there have been times when I was not so happy. I have learned to appreciate those days, too, because they shaped me into the person I am today. The sorrows and struggles gave me strength, and I am thankful for every lesson along the way. I appreciate all my great teachers that I have come across, from the time I was five years old until the present, because each one left me with wisdom I could carry forward. And even now, I remind myself: I always have room for growing.

But at my core, I am a very happy woman, blessed with a loving husband—Leandrew—who loves me unconditionally. I am not dissatisfied, nor empty, in any form of my life. I am truly blessed and full of love.

One Man's Dream was born out of love and inspiration for my husband. I watched him every day as he worked on what he loved most, never giving up on his vision. He poured himself into creating this board game, piece by piece, until one day, together, we put together the first prototype. I will never forget the way his eyes lit up as he finally held a physical game in his hands—something he could see, feel, and share with the world.

But we also knew the reality: the security and protection needed for such a powerful concept in the board game industry were overwhelming. Time and again, we heard that his creation was beyond its time—an idea no one else had thought of yet. And so, we began to dream even bigger.

We realized that transforming his concept into a movie would be the best way to introduce it to the world.

That is when my husband wrote *From East Falls to Hollywood: The World-Wide Swap & Trade / The Gift Challenge*—a story crafted like a movie script, bringing his vision to life. And through that process, I was inspired to write this book, *One Man's Dream: The World-Wide Swap & Trade / The Gift Challenge*. This is not only his story, but ours. It is a story of family, faith, and vision. It is a testimony to perseverance, love, and legacy.

I believe my husband has discovered something truly great, and now it is time to share it with the world. Positive thinking still works, and I hold fast to the five things necessary to a better life: **think, learn, try, work, and believe.** When you do these things with purpose, you will be successful in life.

And above all, remember this truth: *there is only one you, and nobody else can do it like you.*

TABLE OF CONTENTS

INTRODUCTION
THE SPARK OF A DREAM

It all started on a long stretch of highway somewhere between Pennsylvania and Georgia. Leandrew Baillum, known to his family and friends as "Lee," sat behind the wheel of his 18-wheeler, eyes locked on the road, hands steady, and thoughts racing. The hum of the engine served as a soundtrack to his ideas, each mile rolling beneath him like a heartbeat syncing with the rhythm of his dream.

Lee was not just a truck driver. He was a thinker. A doer. A believer. And for years, he had been quietly sketching the outline of a game — not just any game, but a challenge that would unite people across states, across cities, across generations. A game that would inspire trading, sharing, and giving. A game that would bring families together, build community, and reward generosity. In the cab of his truck, he jotted notes in a weathered notebook — dog-eared pages filled with doodles, token systems, and game titles that never felt quite right. But this time, something clicked.

He whispered aloud, "The World-Wide Swap and Trade... The Gift Challenge."

It hit him like a jolt. He grabbed his phone, opened the voice memo app, and started recording. "Gameplay idea: Each player starts with 5,000 personalized coins. The goal is to complete city lots — 1,000 unique coins from a single city. Ten lots complete a state. Winning all fifty states earns you a seat in the annual Gift Challenge finale. Tokens represent more than points — they represent real gifts, community stories, **and legacy**. Each trade is strategic and symbolic."

He paused, then added with conviction, "Not just a game. A movement." The road stretched on, but his vision was crystal clear.

By the time he made it home to Duluth, Georgia, the notebook was overflowing. Lee walked through the front door of the Baillum home, kissed his wife Laura, and said with a spark in his eye, "I think I've finally got it."

Laura, used to Lee's bursts of brilliance, smiled warmly. "Show me."

CHAPTER ONE
THE DREAM REVEALED

Duluth, Georgia — 4:30 A.M.

The vintage twin-bell alarm clock rattled violently, slicing through the still silence of the early morning. Its ring was not just a call to wake up; it was a call to build, to create, to *dream*.

Lee's eyes blinked open.

Nude, as always, he sat up slowly in the middle of his Posturepedic mattress; his body was still, but his mind was racing.

He swung his long, muscular legs over the side of the bed, feet meeting the cool wooden floor. Reaching for his 8-oz bottle of purified water, he twisted the cap with a firm grip. His forearm flexed, revealing every carved line of tendon and control. He drank deeply. It was a ritual.

Hydration before exertion. Clarity before creativity.

In the mirror, he saw what others saw: a six-foot-two man of strength, discipline, and age-earned power. Salt and pepper fade. Goatee is just a whisper away from full silver. Hazel eyes that shifted hue depending on his mood — or his shirt. But that reflection wasn't what mattered.

What mattered was the vision. And this morning, the vision had evolved.

As he stretched, arms grazing the low ceiling, an idea pulsed into place. **The reload cycle. The token economy. The swap system. The Gift.**

How do players stay invested without turning it into just another cash grab?

The question ignited him.

He grabbed his notepad — the worn one with coffee stains and dog-eared pages — and started scribbling:

"Initial Tokens: 2,500

Reload 1: 1,250

Reload 2: 625

Reload 3: 312

Reload 4: 156

Cycle resets after Tier 5.

To restart: complete the challenge or give away a Legacy Gift. No exceptions." He circled the phrase twice:

NO EXCEPTIONS

***

Laura stood in front of the kitchen island, still in her silk robe, nursing a mug of chamomile tea. Her eyes flicked up as Lee came in, notebook under one arm, intensity on his face.

"You didn't sleep again?" she asked. Just woke up with clarity."

She raised an eyebrow. "More clarity than yesterday? Or the day before that?" Lee smiled. "Better. I cracked the cycle problem. Tokens. Reloads. Tier gates."

Laura sighed — half in admiration, half in concern. She had seen this energy before. Bursts of genius followed by days of obsession. She loved his ambition, but she feared the cost.

"I want to show you something," he said, flipping the notebook open in front of her. "Players cannot just hoard tokens. They must *earn* the right to keep playing. Each time they reload, they get half. Until the fifth reload."

CHAPTER TWO
THE AWAKENING

Friday – 5:00 A.M.

The soft golden glow from the hallway nightlight filtered into the bedroom. Lee stirred slightly, eyes fluttering open. He glanced at the clock on the nightstand.

5:00 A.M.

"Dang, I slept in."

He sat up quickly, still energized from the deep sleep and last night's creative rush. He moved with quiet purpose toward the bathroom, splashing water on his face, brushing his teeth, and mentally running through the day's to-do list.

Back in the bedroom, he reached into the dresser and began layering up his workout gear — compression performance leggings, 9-inch freedom running shorts, a Pro Cool Dri-Fit black shirt that hugged his frame, and his well-worn but trusted Air Max Dynasty sneakers.

Laura rolled over, still wrapped in their satin sheets, her eyes slowly opening.

"Mmm… baby," she murmured, taking in the sight of him, "you should be doing YouTube videos for Nike. You wear those garments like they were made just for you."

Lee chuckled, shaking his head modestly. "Thank you, hun," he replied, smiling as he reached for his Dr. Dre Beats Solo 2 headphones and strapped on his running watch.

With a wink, he headed downstairs.

Outside their quiet suburban home in Duluth, Georgia, the morning air was crisp and still. Lee stood in the driveway and dropped into a few warm-up moves — plank push-ups, forward lunges, and sidestep squats. His breath was steady, his focus sharp.

Then, he was off.

From **Whitehead Road** to **Leveled Creek**, cutting across **West Price**, then onto **North Price**, looping back — every step was a beat, a rhythm, a prayer.

But his mind was nowhere near the pavement.

He was deep in thought — envisioning how *The Gift* could become more than an app. *"Imagine it on Xbox. PlayStation. Real-world missions. Multiplayer trades. Epic family adventures…"*

He could see players creating real impact through storytelling and action. He imagined siblings teaming up, couples competing, strangers bonding through trades that carried heart.

The possibilities were endless.

By the time he returned home, sweat clinging to his brow and inspiration coursing through his veins, he was already drafting ideas in his head for game expansions. His steps slowed as he neared the front door.

"Now it's time to get ready for work…" he thought.

***

6:20 A.M.

Back upstairs, Lee peeled off his workout gear and stepped into the large walk-in shower. As warm water cascaded down his back, he leaned forward, resting one hand against the tile. It was a moment of peace, of grounding. He reached for his Lacoste Croc solid black washcloth and applied a quarter-size amount of AXE Dark Temptation body wash.

He was just beginning to lather his body when he heard the soft *click* of the bathroom door. Then, Laura's gentle voice:

"Honey… May I join you in the shower?"

Lee smiled, eyes still closed. He loved that she asked. That small act of respect touched something deep in him — the mutual reverence, quiet trust, the knowing.

She stepped into the shower slowly, the steam rising between them like smoke from a flame. Without a word, she took the washcloth from his hands and began to gently caress his back, her fingers gliding over his muscles, his shoulders, his lower spine.

Her hands were soft, precise — washing, massaging, teasing. She moved lower, over his thighs, calves, then turned him around to face her. Her lips found his neck, then his collarbone. She traced his forearms with her fingertips and cleaned every inch of his body with love.

When she knelt to kiss his abdomen, her tongue slipped inside his navel, and Lee inhaled sharply. A quiet gasp escaped his lips as his body responded to her touch, his every nerve ending alert, alive.

For long minutes, they moved together in slow, steamy passion — a dance that only they knew the rhythm too. Every touch was a memory, every kiss a promise. When their lips met again in a deep, lingering kiss, it sealed the moment — not just physical, but emotional, spiritual.

She turned in his arms, and he wrapped himself around her, whispering her name as the water poured down their entwined bodies. At that moment, time slowed.

"Lee…" she breathed. "Lee…"

"Lee…"

Afterward, they stayed wrapped in each other, heartbeats slowing in unison. He rested his head on her shoulder and whispered, "I love you, Laura."

She looked up, tears of joy soft in her eyes. "I love you, Lee. You make me feel desired. Happy. Whole."

***

7:20 A.M.

Showered and refreshed, Lee dried off in the bedroom. His work clothes were pressed and laid out across the bed — hunter green boxer briefs, dark blue Dickies work pants, a white crew neck tee, and a short-sleeved light blue button-down. His navy Dickies jacket and steel-toe boots sat by the door.

His lunch, like always, was packed and ready for him — Laura's quiet love language. He kissed her tenderly before he left. "See you later, my love."

"Be safe," she said, smiling, "and go do great things."

Lee stepped outside, climbed into his 2015 Chevrolet Equinox SUV, and drove off toward his workday.

But his mind was still on the game. On the movement.

On *The Gift*.

CHAPTER THREE
SEEDS OF BELIEF

Monday – 6:45 A.M.

A cool November morning in Duluth, Georgia

The scent of fresh-brewed coffee drifted through the kitchen. The windows fogged slightly from the warmth inside, brushing against the brisk air outside. Lee sat at the kitchen table, a yellow legal pad in front of him, pen tapping the margin.

Across from him, Laura stirred a spoon of raw sugar into her mug. She watched him — thoughtful, focused — the way she always did when he got like this.

Lee leaned forward, folding his hands together.

"Babe," he began, "I have been building this board game on my computer and in my head for years now. It is time I finally give it shape."

Laura looked up. "The Gift?" she asked.

He nodded. "The *World-Wide Swap and Trade…* slash *The Gift.*" A pause. "It is more than a game, Laura. Way more."

She set her cup down. "Tell me."

Lee took a breath, then the words flowed like water — calm, clear, unwavering.

"It is a social network game, yes — but not just for entertainment. It is for education, skill building, therapy, healing, and expression. It is about connections. Real connection."

He leaned back slightly, eyes shining with conviction.

"I want kids to learn about value. I want teens to express their creativity. I want adults to find something human again. I want families to play together. Strangers become friends. I want this to move from a board game to a portable video game and eventually make it to the big screen, further up the chain of command into a Netflix series, then into real life."

Laura studied him. "So, it's like… more than trading things?"

"Exactly," Lee said, growing more animated. "It is about trading meaning. Every swap has a story. Every gift leaves a fingerprint. People do not just get stuff — they get experience, they gain understanding, they feel seen."

He slid the notebook across the table.

"There'll be a token system. Five-token sets, one set per swap. But here's the key: you can't just *buy* progress. You collect tokens from people — real people. Every lot has to be earned." She looked down at the notes:

5 tokens per set

1,000-token lots = full milestone. Collect from 200 players to complete the lot

Save meaningful stories. Unlock the vault.

Laura smiled. "This is brilliant, Lee. But… this is going to take time, resources, testing, programming…"

"I know," he said, "but I believe it is essential for the world. She reached across the table, placing her hand over his.

"Well then," she said softly, "you have me. Let us start building it."

***

Later That Morning

On the Road to Savannah, Georgia

The diesel engine of Lee's 18-wheeler roared to life as he merged onto I-95 North. The sun had risen, casting a soft glow over the asphalt, and the cool air had a bite to it — just the way he liked it.

Lee's thoughts circled as the miles stretched ahead. He was used to the hum of the road, but his thoughts stayed fixed on *The Gift*.

"How do I make the token collection feel real? Not like a cheap badge — but a badge of honor." He replayed his conversation with Laura in his mind. Her support was like oxygen — it gave breath to his vision.

"What if you could not just collect tokens from one person? You had to connect with hundreds to build a lot…"

He imagined the mechanics:

A **lot** = 1,000 tokens

Each player can give up five tokens.

You need **two hundred players** to complete a full lot.

Tokens earned only through accepted swaps or **Gift Stories** (where you tell the why behind the trade)

"Limitless items can be uploaded," he murmured aloud, "but the best ones will not be easy to get. Players will have to hustle. Think. Care."

He pictured a leaderboard — not ranked by wealth or speed, but by **"Legacy Swaps."** The ones that changed lives. The ones people talked about in the comments. Trades that taught lessons.

This was not just a board game anymore; it's much more. It was a movement.

It was testimony.

It was a bridge between giving and growing.

Lee tightened his grip on the wheel, eyes locked on the road ahead, but his mind had already traveled miles beyond it.

CHAPTER FOUR
ROOTS, WINGS, AND LEGACY

Back home in Duluth, Georgia, Laura moved gracefully through the rhythm of the day—folding clothes, answering emails, dinner half-prepped. She thrived in this balance, taking care of what mattered most: her family.

Upstairs, sunlight poured through the window onto Lee's vision board while soft jazz played in the background. Though he was not home yet, his presence filled the house—in every book on the shelf, every quote taped to the fridge, every heartbeat in the walls, the air was filled with love of family.

The Sons Who Carried the Torch

Their son Rodney, known as RJ, had recently graduated from a four-year university where he played basketball—his first love. At six-foot-three with a lean, athletic build and a dark, hustle haircut that framed his smooth caramel skin, RJ embodied both strength and softness. From an early age, he was drawn to people's pain, their needs, their healing. So, it made sense when he chose to major in Physics and Medicine. Now, he has worked as a **Biophysicist**, diagnosing disease and collaborating with physicians in the hospital labs, steady, sharp, and compassionate. Their son Leandrew, affectionately called LJ, stood six-foot-two with a mocha taper fade that always looked freshly shaped. LJ had never been one to follow the crowd. While others chased trends, he pursued justice. That pursuit led him to complete seven years of law school and become a **Criminal Defense Attorney**, committed to defending those who thought they could never afford proper representation. He believed in justice for all, not a selected few with money. "Everyone deserves a voice," LJ had once told his father. "Even the forgotten."

Lee often said with pride, "I may only hold their hands for a little while, but I'll hold their hearts forever."

He raised his sons to understand that adulthood and being a man were more than muscle or money—it was responsibility. He taught them three rules that would never fail:

Protect your roof.

Keep the lights on.

Keep the fridge full.

"If those are taken care of," Lee would say, "everything else will fall into place."

The Daughters Who Built Their Own Paths

Lee and Laura also shared four daughters—**Diane, Antoinette, Brenda, and Brenda**. Yes, the family had two Brendas, and both carried the name with pride. Each daughter was raised to be bold, brilliant, and beautifully grounded.

Though they now live in different parts of the states, West Virginia, Pennsylvania, Minnesota and Texas, their connection to home remained unshakable.

From early on, Lee and Laura taught them not just to speak up, but to speak with purpose. Whenever questions arose, the answer wasn't handed to them. Instead, they were told, "Research it. Bring us back a game plan."

That discipline carried into their adult lives. Each daughter pursued courses in Communication and Technology, eventually earning degrees in **Communication Studies**. Today, they lead in powerful positions—Healthcare Communication Manager, Training & Development Specialist, Corporate Event Planner, and Crisis Communications Manager. They ran their departments with excellence, living out the principles of faith, family, and perseverance.

The Son-in-Law Who Brought a New Beat

Derrick, aka DJ. Derrick had graduated from **Roman Catholic High School** and immediately stepped into service by joining the **United States Military**. There, he studied as a **Visual Information Specialist and Recording Engineer**, mastering the art of telling stories through images, sound, and design. DJ's discipline, creativity, and commitment carried into the Baillum family seamlessly.

When DJ returned home, he brought not just his military skills, but also a new wave of innovation. He was the one who turned the living room into a sound-mixing hub, syncing music with Lee's game vision, blending beats with trailers, and making sure the world could not only see the dream—but feel it.

The Daughter-in-Law with Vision

Jelisa, a proud graduate of **Girls' High School in Philadelphia**, had always been known for her sharp mind and ability to see the bigger picture. From there, she pursued a **Bachelor of Arts and a degree in Psychology**, equipping her to understand people, guide strategy, and build bridges between vision and execution.

Jelisa wasn't just family by marriage—she was a strategist and motivator. She reminded everyone that *The World-Wide Swap and Trade / The Gift Challenge* wasn't just a game. With her insight into global culture and human behavior, she helped shape it into a **movement**. Her voice often pushed the family to think bigger, plan smarter, and move with confidence.

CHAPTER FIVE
BUILDING THE BLUEPRINT

The warm aroma of baked cornbread and smoked turkey wings filled the house as Lee pulled into the driveway. It had been a long drive back from Massachusetts, but nothing could dim the light in his eyes — not after the ideas that had poured into him on the road. His mind was electric, and he could not wait to share every detail with Laura.

Inside, laughter bounced from room to room. The grandkids were home — all of them. Zahiyah and Ahlaysia were in the living room doing a TikTok routine. Jayla was in the kitchen helping Laura stir the collard greens. Shameer and Rodney were deep into a PlayStation match. Jebrea and Jessica sat at the dining room table drawing, while little Amorah bounced from room to room, the joy of the house in motion.

Lee opened the front door with a deep sigh of contentment. "I'm home!" he called.

From the kitchen, Laura appeared, wiping her hands directly on a towel. "There he is," she smiled. "The man with the master plan."

Lee grinned and held up his notebook. "I've got something for you, baby."

***

Later that evening, after dinner was cleared and the little ones were tucked in, a quiet atmosphere Lee and Laura sat at the kitchen table. His notebook lay open between them, pages full of scribbles, arrows, sketches, and bold ideas.

"I've been thinking about everything," Lee began. "The game, the mechanics, how to get people engaged… not just to play, but to stay. To believe in it."

Laura leaned in, listening intently as he walked her through his vision.

"There will be five-token sets. You earn them through meaningful swaps. Each swap comes with a story — a Gift Story. You collect from two hundred different players to build a 'lot.' A lot is 1,000 tokens."

Laura nodded, impressed. "So, it encourages community. And not just hoarding things — it is about connection."

"Exactly," Lee said. "Each player can upload their own city, state, and a photo when they sign on. We are going to cover all fifty states, city by city. Eventually, I want this thing on Xbox, PS4, PS5, even a CD-ROM for computers."

Laura's eyes lit up. "That is big. That is brilliant. And you are not alone in this — you have got us."

Just then, Zahiyah peeked in. "What are y'all working on?"

Lee gestured for her to come over. "Come here, baby girl. Bring it, everyone. I want your help." Within minutes, the table was full — Ahlaysia and Jayla with their sketchpads, Shameer with his laptop, Jebrea and Jessica ready with colors, Rodney spinning ideas, and little Amorah crawling into Laura's lap.

Lee looked around the table — his tribe. His legacy.

"Alright," he said. "I'm building a game. *The World-Wide Swap and Trade / The Gift*. And I want you to help me build it from the ground up."

The kids' eyes widened.

Jayla raised her hand. "Can we make characters?"

"Avatars," Lee corrected with a smile. "Yes. Create what you think your player should look like."

Zahiyah was already sketching. "Mine's going to wear braids and a bomber jacket!"
"Can we add pets?" asked Jessica.

"Sure can," said Lee.

"Can our swaps be like... digital treasure chests?" added Shameer.

Rodney was writing. "What if certain items unlock bonuses — like a Golden Swap that connects you to a player in a different country?"

Lee could not stop smiling. "Now you are thinking globally. This is exactly what I needed." Amorah reached over and touched one of the sketches. "This one's pretty, Daddy."

He kissed her forehead. "Just like you."

***

'By the time the clock hit 11:30 PM, the table was covered in drawings, character names, mock-ups, and color-coded swap ideas. There were piles of tokens sketched on index cards, hand-drawn maps of cities, and page after page of swap story prompts.

Laura looked at Lee, her eyes soft with pride. "You've started something real here." Lee took her hand. "We've started it. All of us."

And as the family finally packed up for bed, Lee stood back and looked at the table once more. It did not look like paper and pencil anymore.

It looked like a movement beginning to breathe.

CHAPTER SIX
THE STRATEGY CIRCLE

The morning sun shone gently through the curtains as the scent of hazelnut coffee drifted through the house. Lee stood at the kitchen counter, flipping through his notebook with purpose. Last night, he had given him everything — laughter, sketches, mock-ups, tokens, avatars, ideas from the kids that even he hadn't thought of.

But now it was time to **build the blueprint into a real launch strategy.**

Laura stepped into the kitchen wearing her reading glasses, coffee mug in hand, and her usual calm-but-ready-to-lead presence.

"You ready, strategist?" she asked with a grin.

Lee leaned over and kissed her forehead. "Let's build."

***

By 10:00 A.M., the large dining room table was "transformed "into a **strategy war room**. Sticky notes lined the walls. Laura had organized whiteboards into labeled sections: *Vision, Audience, Platform, Distribution, Marketing,* and *Funding.*

She poured herself and Lee a second cup of coffee.

"Alright, first," Laura said, tapping her marker to the board. "Let us define the user. For whom is this game?"

Lee answered confidently. "Families. Dreamers. Students. Creators. Givers. People who want more out of social connection than likes and views. People who want to feel purpose again." She nodded. "Good. Let us structure that into age ranges and device use. Tablets, phones, consoles, computers."

Just then, the front door opened. In walked **RJ** and **LJ**, their stride smooth, eyes alert — young men aware they had been invited into something big.

"Morning, folks," said RJ, placing his laptop on the table. "You called in the tech squad?" "You know it," said Lee. "We're building this thing brick by brick."

RJ opened his laptop. "Let me show you what is possible for server-side development. You are going to need cloud hosting, real-time data sync, and a layered security model to protect users' personal info. Especially if it is going to be social and interactive."

LJ chimed in. "And from a legal perspective, you will need user agreements, privacy policies, and copyrighted content protected. You're starting a business and a digital product line at the same time."

Lee sat back, impressed. "This is why I'm glad y'all are mine."

***

An hour later, four more voices entered the circle: *Brenda, BreBre, Tudy and Dee,* arms full of folders and printouts.

"Sorry, we're late," said Dee, "we were up all night looking through app incubators and pitch competitions."

"Y'all came prepared?" Laura asked.

BreBre grinned. "Of course. We found three startup grants, two crowdfunding platforms like I Fund Women and Kickstarter, plus an accelerator in Atlanta that helps launch Black-owned tech ideas."

Laura raised her eyebrows. "That's real."

Lee looked at his wife. "Told you we're building something the world's never seen." They spread out the papers on the table.

Dee pointed to one. "This one will give you $50,000 in seed funding if you're accepted. But you'll need a visual prototype and a video pitch."

Laura glanced around the room. "Then we'd better get started."

***

By mid-afternoon, a team was formally assembled.

Lee & Laura – Founders. Creative + Strategic Leads

RJ – Tech Consultant & Data Analyst

LJ– Legal Advisor & Compliance Lead

BreBre & **Tudy** – Research & Grant Writing

Dee & Brenda – Platform Funding & Pitch Development

The Kids – User Testing & Visual Creation Team. They called themselves:

Team Gifted

Lee closed his notebook. "This isn't just a game anymore." Laura smiled. "It's a movement."

RJ raised his glass of sweet tea. "To connect." LJ added, "To purpose."

And together, they toasted.

To The World-Wide Swap and Trade / The Gift Challenge

CHAPTER SEVEN
THE HEART OF THE HOME

The sun was just starting to lower itself behind the treetops of Duluth, Georgia, as Laura pulled into the driveway. Her errands for the day were complete — bills paid, pantry restocked, and bags from the local market filled with fresh produce and everything she needed for a warm, soulful dinner.

Tonight's menu was one of Lee's favorites: **liver and onions**, seasoned exactly right, served with fluffy **white rice**, tender **collard greens**, golden **cornbread**, and a tall pitcher of her signature **homemade lemonade** — tangy and sweet. For dessert, Lee had baked a rich, moist **pineapple upside-down cake**, its caramelized topping glistening like a memory from back home.

Laura moved with ease through the kitchen, humming quietly as pots simmered, the oven clicked off, and the aroma of tradition filled the air.

***

Upstairs, the house was alive in its usual after-school symphony. Kids were everywhere —in their rooms, others on the phone, in the basement, or lingering in the backyard. The sounds of laughter, gaming, and music wove into the house like threads of family life.

Lee had just come in from a long day on the road. After a quick kiss hello, he slipped into the bathroom for a hot shower, letting the steam and water wash off the miles of the highway.

Back downstairs, Laura found herself with a rare, precious **fifteen minutes** to herself.

She made her way into the family room, heading straight for her sanctuary — the **brown leather recliner** by the window, its nail head trim wrapping around the arms like a touch of elegance from another era. She pulled up the footrest, grabbed her **plush, marshmallow-white throw blanket**, and settled in.

Beside her sat a tall-stemmed wine glass filled with **'94 Du Bellay red**, a rare indulgence she only allowed herself when she genuinely wanted to unwind.

She reached for her book — *"The Coldest Winter Ever"* by Sister Souljah — but before she opened the cover, her gaze wandered out the window.

Her mind drifted.

Back in time.

***

She was a little girl again, sitting in the back seat of her parents' car as they pulled up to **Grandma Daisy Long's house** for Sunday dinner. She could almost smell the baked macaroni, the ham glazed in brown sugar, the sweet potato pie cooling on the sill. Her aunts, uncles, cousins, and neighbors — all gathered around the long table, telling stories and laughing between bites.

Those family dinners were sacred. And though Grandma Daisy had long passed, Laura had vowed to keep that tradition alive.

"You always remember the good times growing up," she often told her kids.

"And dinner together — that's where love lives."

At **6:45 P.M.**, Laura took a slow sip of her wine, savoring the moment of stillness. Then she heard footsteps.

Lee appeared, freshly showered, dressed in his **athletic sweat cargo pants**, his skin still warm from the steam. Without saying a word, he walked over to her and leaned down, placing a hot, lingering kiss on her full, soft lips — the kind of kiss that spoke volumes about love, desire, and everything in between.

"I love you, hun," Laura whispered with a gentle smile.

"I love you more," Lee replied, brushing a curl away from her face. "Dinner ready?" "You know it."

***

Laura called out from the kitchen: "Alright, everybody — dinner time!"

Within minutes, feet were flying down the stairs and voices rang out across the house. The family gathered around the dining room table, already laid out with dishes that filled the air with comfort and soul.

Lee took his usual seat at the head of the table, looked around at the family, then bowed his head. "Our Heavenly Father," he began,

"We thank you for this food we are about to receive.

We thank you for keeping our family safe and bringing us together. We thank you for allowing us to see another day —

So give us grace. Amen."

Plates of dinner passed, laughter returned, and the kitchen transformed into a room of **love, flavor, and stories**.

Everyone shared how their day had gone — from schoolwork to innovative ideas, updates on college projects to a funny moment in the yard. These dinners were not just meals. They were **connections to the family.** It was the glue that held the Baillum family together.

***

At **9:00 P.M.**, cleanup began. Everyone chipped in — clearing plates, wiping counters, loading the dishwasher, and taking out the trash. In no time, the kitchen was spotless, the dining room table cleared, and the night winding down.

Lee and Laura moved into the living room, side by side on the **leather couch** they had picked out together years ago. Laura curled into his side.

"How was your day?" she asked.

Lee smiled. "Let me tell you about the ideas that hit me while I was driving. Hold on, let me grab my paper — I wrote it all down, so I will not forget."

He got up and returned with a stack of scribbled notes and napkin sketches, flipping to a page in his notebook as he sat back beside her.

"It's been three days since I've been home," Lee said. "But I swear, baby, when I am on that road, I miss you more than anything. Just being back here, sharing ideas with you like we always do — that's my peace."

Laura touched his hand, squeezing it gently.

"That's what makes us work," she said. "We love, we listen, we build… together."

And with that, Lee began to tell her all about the new features for **The World-Wide Swap and Trade / The Gift Challenge** that had come to him on the road — while outside, the house glowed from within, full of laughter, warmth, and dreams being born.

CHAPTER EIGHT
DREAMS, DECISIONS, AND DEDICATION

It was well past dinner, and the warmth of the evening lingered in the air. The house was calm now—dishes put away, conversations from the day settled into memories. In the living room, Lee and Laura wrapped in each other's company, still unpacking all the dreams Lee had carried with him during his long days on the road.

He leaned forward, energized by his thoughts.

"Laura," he said, his voice rich with possibility, "I want *The World-Wide Swap and Trade / The Gift Challenge* to be more than just a game—it must be a *movement*. A chance for people to win life-changing prizes. I'm talking about **houses, cars, paid-off credit, dream vacations,** even **medical bills erased** and **furnished homes delivered with the key in hand.**"

Laura's eyes lit up. She could already see the vision forming clearly in her mind.

"You know what that means for people?" she asked. "That means *hope*. That means new beginnings."

Lee nodded. "Exactly. We will create rewards so appealing and impactful to people's lives that it will attract people from all over the world, they will be drawn in—not just to play—but to dream."

***

The clock on the wall ticked gently to **10:00 P.M.**

Laura stretched and smiled. "Come on, honey. It is time to retire for the night." Lee grinned as they headed upstairs. "Rest? After the way I am feeling right now?" Laura laughed softly. "Just get in the shower."

They stepped into the warmth of the water, steam rising around them like a quiet symphony. Their connection—rooted in years of loyalty, laughter, and love—was undeniable. Whenever they were alone, it felt like their first time all over again. Each tentative touch was filled with meaning. Lee was gentle, intentional, and so deeply attentive to Laura's needs. And Laura—romantic, tender, and endlessly loving—listened to every word Lee said, supported every dream he shared.

They were more than a couple. They were partners in every sense. And to everyone who knew them—including Lee's best friend Will—they were the **Power**

Couple. Will had dubbed them the first time he met Laura, back in the Eastfalls Projects where he and Lee grew up. " The Power Couple"

"Man," Will had said, watching the two of them together, "you have got a real one. Y'all gonna move mountains together."

***

The next morning, Lee rose early, careful not to wake Laura, who lay still in peaceful sleep. After last night's passion, he knew she deserved every moment of rest.

He went through his usual routine: freshened up, slipped on his **Nike running gear**, grabbed his **Beats Solo 2 headphones**, and slipped quietly out the door.

His run lasted just over an hour. With every stride down the quiet streets of Suwanee, Lee felt the ideas inside him stretch and breathe. His game, his legacy, his love for his family, all of it fueled his steps.

By the time he returned, Laura was up and radiant. She had already showered, dressed, and was standing in the kitchen cooking **his favorite breakfast**—scrambled eggs, smoked turkey sausage, wheat toast, and avocado slices. And, as always, she was planning dinner before lunch had even started.

Cooking dinner **every day** was something she took pride in. For Laura, nourishing her family's bodies and souls was part of her calling.

***

Around **1:00 P.M.**, a familiar knock came at the door.

It was **Ahlaysia**, graceful and focused, holding something unspoken in her heart. "Can I talk to you and Grandpa for a moment?" she asked.

"Of course," Laura replied with a smile, motioning her in.

The three of them took seats around the **round dining room table**, a place sacred to the Baillum family. This was where real conversations "were built"—sometimes heated, sometimes healing, but always honest.

Laura gently prompted, "Okay, baby. You have the floor. What is on your mind?" Ahlaysia looked nervous. "Please don't be mad."

"You know I could never be mad at you," Laura replied calmly. "That's why we talk—to understand each other."

There was a pause. A heavy silence. Then Ahlaysia said it.

"I don't want to go to college."

The room stilled. You could hear a pin drop. Five full minutes passed.

That was Laura's way—**let them feel the weight of their words**, let them think. Lee leaned toward his wife and asked gently, "Hun, are you going to say anything?"

"Give me a minute," Laura answered, her eyes never leaving Ahlaysia.

Education was a cornerstone of the Baillum household. Laura and Lee had raised their children and grandchildren to be **accountable, driven,** and **disciplined**. They believed in earning everything, expecting nothing handed, and never quitting halfway.

Finally, Laura spoke.

"So, what is your plan, baby? I know you did not come to that decision without thinking it through. Tell me."

***

Ahlaysia took a deep breath.

"I want to work in **beauty and fashion**. I have an eye for it. I see things others do not. I want to become a **platform artist**."

She paused, then added, "But not just for anyone. I want to work for **Bobby Daughter's Hair Line**."

Laura's heart stopped for a second.

That was **her** company—**her brand**, her tribute to her beloved father **Robert Long**, known by all as *Bobby*. The company produced handmade oils, wig hats, and custom wigs. The name itself was a legacy. And now, her granddaughter wanted to carry it forward.

Laura composed herself, then said, "So what is your plan? How are you going to make that dream real?"

Ah'laysia had straightened up; her voice was strong now. "I am going to go to **trade school**. I am going to learn everything—hair coloring, haircutting for every face shape, and styles for every texture. I will master scalp treatments, learn about conditions like alopecia, ringworm, dermatitis, and how to keep my clients safe and confident."

Laura blinked, impressed by the detail. "You've done your homework."

"Yes, ma'am. And I want to work side-by-side with *you*, Grandma. I want to walk in your footsteps. You have taught me so much, and I know my great-grandfather would be proud."

Lee chuckled, breaking the intensity. "Okay, Laura, do not scare the child with all those medical terms. She gets the point."

They all laughed.

Then Laura stood, walked around the table, and wrapped Ahlaysia in a hug. "I love you, baby. And if this is truly your passion, then we will support your decision **110 percent**. Just promise me you will work and take it seriously."

"I will," Ahlaysia whispered. "I promise."

Just then, little **Amorah** burst into the room with a bright smile, shouting, "I love you, Mommom!" as she wrapped herself around Laura's leg.

It was one of those simple, tender, unforgettable moments.

In that dining room, three generations of visionaries sat shoulder to shoulder—building dreams, handing down legacies, and reminding one another that **no dream is too small**, **no path too** different, and family is the foundation of everything.

CHAPTER NINE
THE MOCK-UP SESSION

It was a crisp Saturday morning, the kind that carried both energy and clarity. The Baillum household was abuzz with excitement. The dining room table was full of laptops that were all plugged in, notebooks stacked high, and the aroma of fresh cinnamon rolls, bacon, and hazelnut coffee filled the air.

Today was not just a regular Saturday; it was "the day."

It was **Mock-up Session Day** — the beginning of something *real*. The day Lee had dreamed about for years.

Laura, clipboard in hand, was organizing the morning flow like a seasoned executive producer. "Okay," she said, looking around at the room full of eager faces, "Let's make this vision visible."

***

RJ and **LJ** were the first to arrive. Dressed casually but focused, they brought their technical and legal insight to the table. RJ had a notepad full of planning and server ideas, while LJ, the criminal attorney, brought up user agreements, liability safeguards, and privacy protocols.

"This can't just *look* good," LJ said firmly, "It has to *work* safely."

BreBre and **Dee** were next. Armed with tablets and styluses, they were deep in their research on funding platforms. From Kickstarter to GoFundMe, small business grants, and app launch sponsors — they had options lined up, complete with pros and cons.

"We'll pitch this in phases," Dee said. "First beta, then full expansion, then licensing partnerships. Think of the long game."

***

Zahiyah, Ahlaysia, Shameer, Jayla, Jebrea, Rodney, Jessica, and **Amorah** trickled in shortly after, taking seats like a well-formed creative squad. Each of them was assigned a specific creative lane:

Zahiyah and **Jayla** managed avatar development, crafting characters that players from around the world could relate to — diverse, stylish, and empowering.

Shameer and **Rodney** focused on map layouts — visualizing how players would move through cities, swap items, trade tokens, and unlock regions.

Jebrea and **Jessica** were the strategy and color team, developing themes, user interfaces, and game reward tier designs.

Amorah, still young but brimming with imagination, helped with sound effects and catchphrases. Her favorite? *"Swap it. Trade it. Gift it."*

***

At the center of it all sat **Lee**, marker in hand, drawing diagrams on the whiteboard.

"We are building a challenge system that mirrors *real-life value exchange*, right? So, players need to be able to swap tangible or digital items with each other — sneakers, vinyl, exclusive merch, digital artwork, you name it."

He turned to the board and continued. "We need five token levels, each unlocking access to new swap categories. Let us color-code them—Gold, Ruby, Emerald, Sapphire, and Onyx."

Laura leaned in, adding, "And we will build in a *Gift Zone*, where players can donate or 'gift' items to earn legacy points. That is what sets this apart — the *giving* part. You give; you grow."

***

The energy in the room was electric.

RJ proposed encrypted barcodes for every tradeable item to ensure traceability and fairness. LJ was already outlining a fair-use disclaimer to protect users. BreBre found a grant designed for digital creatives launching social connection platforms. Dee had mock emails drafted to potential sponsors.

And then it was time for the first reveal.

Zahiyah clicked her laptop and projected her first avatar onto the screen — a tall character named "Legacy Lee" with twist-out locs, a sleek bomber jacket, and a confident stance. The room applauded.

Then Jayla revealed "Lady Swap"—a bold, stylish, globally inspired female avatar wearing hoop earrings, tech glasses, and a scarf tied around her locs.

"That's fire," Lee said, genuinely impressed. "We're just getting started," Jayla replied.

***

By lunchtime, the Baillum house had transformed into a design studio. Music played softly in the background, and everywhere you looked, creativity flowed: sketchpads, mood boards, digital mock-ups, code snippets, and vision statements.

Lee stood back for a moment, taking it all in. This was more than a family meeting. This was **a legacy being born**.

***

As the session wrapped for the day, Laura passed out plates of honey-baked chicken, mac and cheese, and cabbage she had prepared earlier, and they ate as a family, still bouncing ideas off each other between bites.

And as the sun began to set, Lee looked around the table, his heart full.

He stood and said, "We are not just building a game. We are building something that'll change lives. This—right here—this is *The Gift*."

Everyone raised their glass of lemonade. They echoed. "To The Gift"

And with that, **The World-Wide Swap and Trade / The Gift Challenge** moved from concept to creation — one mock-up at a time.

CHAPTER TEN
THE TEST RUN

As the Baillum family prepared to run their first in-house simulation of *The World-Wide Swap and Trade / The Gift Challenge*, laughter echoed through the home. Tablets were charged. Mock trades were queued. Avatars were loading, and Real-time gifting scenarios had been mapped out across dry-erase boards and digital dashboards.

But then, there was noise coming from the front door. The key turned slowly.

Everyone went silent.

Nobody was expecting company, and only the family had keys. Lee's instincts kicked in instantly.

As the protector of his home by any means necessary, he moved swiftly toward the door, his jaw tight and his right hand curled, ready—just in case.

As the knob turned and the door cracked open, Lee drew back, heart steady but alert. And then he paused.

His eyes widened.

There stood **Derrick**, his son —better known to the family as **DJ**.

***

DJ, dressed in his military fatigues, stepped into the doorway with a proud, confident smile that stretched across his clean-shaven face.

"DJ?" Lee said, his voice cracking with emotion.

"Surprise, Dad," DJ replied with a smirk. "RJ and LJ told me everything—about the game, the mock-up session, and how the family's coming together to build something legendary. I could not miss this."

The room erupted.

Laura gasped and held her hands over her mouth before hurrying over to hug him tight. The kids screamed in joy. Jayla started crying. Jebrea ran to grab his favorite plate. Amorah yelled, "Uncle DJ!"

The hugs, laughter, and warmth poured over DJ like a homecoming should.

***

Once everyone was settled, DJ turned to Lee and said, "Dad, you cannot start the mock-up without me. You know my role in the military. I am a **Visual Information Specialist** and **Recording**

Engineer. I bring the sound. I create the vibe. I produce the impact. We are talking about motion graphics, voiceovers, video intros, and cinematic trailers. I mix, primary, and layer digital content—this is what I *do*. Let me help bring this to life."

Lee stood there, visibly moved, his son's presence reminding him why this dream was worth every minute.

DJ looked around the room and declared, "We all have roles to play. And together, we are going to make *The World-Wide Swap and Trade / The Gift Challenge* a global experience. A family that *prays together, stays together*. And we're praying *and* playing—as one—to bring 'One Man's Dream' to life."

***

The mood shifted to high gear.

DJ entered the dining room and immediately got to work. He pulled out his laptop, connected it to the family's speaker system, and loaded up a soundboard filled with effects, theme music, and digital atmospheres. The game sounds like "Swap Locked In," "You've Earned a Gift," and "Next Tier Unlocked!" echoed through the house.

It brought the whole thing to life. The test run officially began.

***

Each family member stepped into their assigned roles:

RJ monitored the server simulation, testing how trades will be sent, received, and logged.

LJ reviewed the "Terms of Use" agreement for gameplay compliance.

BreBre evaluated in-app purchase options for upgrading avatars.

Dee launched the beta crowdfunding page.

Zahiyah and **Jayla** guided the team through the avatar swap features, demonstrating how players could trade accessories and unlock regional costumes.

Shameer, Rodney, Jessica, and **Jebrea** took turns simulating player moves across the 50-state digital map.

Amorah added voiceover lines like "Swap It. Trade It. Gift It." in her adorable, animated voice with Jelisa, her mother; the two were incredible.

And **DJ**? He synchronized it all together—with transitions, motion, and emotion. Lee and Laura stood back, watching their family operate like a startup studio, fueled not just by passion—but by *purpose*.

***

Laura whispered to Lee, "Can you believe this? You dreamed of this moment years ago. Now look…"

Lee nodded, humbled, his eyes glistening. "I believed in it. But watching them believe in it, too? That is what makes it real."

The family test run continued for hours. There were laughs, strategy debates, coding glitches, avatar crashes—and moments of brilliance.

At the end of the night, Laura called everyone into a circle. "Let's pray."

They all held hands.

She said softly, "Lord, we thank you for your vision. We thank you for your unity. Let this dream be more than just a game—let it be a gift that connects families, spreads joy, and changes lives.

Amen."

"Amen," the family echoed. And with that, the test run was complete.

CHAPTER ELEVEN
THE TURNING POINT

It's getting late, and the Baillum household slowly winds down from the day's excitement. After hours of brainstorming, laughing, and evaluating the game prototype, everyone naturally slips into their evening rhythms—each finding a way to unwind.

Down in the kitchen, the brothers—RJ, LJ, and DJ—gather near the island countertop, sipping on ginger ale and cracking jokes like old times.

"Man," RJ says, nudging DJ, "your home. We cannot let the night go to waste."

LJ smirks. "Exactly. You need a little taste of normal life again. Golf club, scary movie, and a good steak from Outback Steakhouse."

DJ grins wide. "Bet. I need that. Let's catch up. I have plenty of stories."

The three of them have a signature family style that they do all of the time, it is called "first bump," and upstairs, they went to get ready.

***

Upstairs in the pink-and-purple loft room, Ahlaysia sits cross-legged on the floor surrounded by spools of fabric, ribbon, rhinestones, and glitter pens. She's helping Jebrea and Amorah design matching outfits for their dolls. It's their version of a mini design studio—complete with music playing from a Bluetooth speaker and mood boards taped to the wall.

"I'm going to sew these together tonight," Ahlaysia says, threading a needle. "Your dolls are going to be runway-ready."

Jebrea beams. "Can mine have glitter shoes?" "You got it."

Amorah claps her hands. "And mine needs a cape! Like a superhero!" Their giggles fill the upstairs hallway, a soundtrack of simple joy.

***

Meanwhile, BreBre, Dee, and Tudy are pulling out of the driveway all dressed up and singing old-school classics in the car. Tonight, they're heading back to Philly for a concert at The Dell Music Center.

"Fantasia, SWV, Patti, AND the Temptations?" Dee shouts from the back seat. "I've been waiting for this since February!"

Tudy steers with one hand, the other up like she's in church. "This is more than a concert—it's therapy!"

BreBre flips her curls and laughs. "Let's hit 95 North like we're in our twenties again." They disappear into the night, bonded by Love, friendship, sisterhood, history and music.

***

Back in the Baillum family media room, Rodney and Shameer are fully immersed in their VR headsets. They are dodging, leaping, and swinging their way through a new game called VR Parkour, their avatars gliding over rooftops and neon-lit platforms.

"Yo Shameer," Rodney says through his headset, "this is how I want our game to feel."

"Exactly!" Shameer replies, panting a little from excitement. "It's got to have that freedom—full immersion."

Rodney pauses the game and pulls up a digital sketchpad. "To get that, we need to help Poppop build The World-Wide Swap and Trade / The Gift Challenge to support cross-platform play." Shameer nods, pulling up a list of supported systems. "We're talking Meta Quest, Pico, PSVR 2, Apple Vision Pro, Xbox Series X/S, SteamVR, PS5, even iPads and Mac. We need full access and cross-play compatibility."

Rodney adds, "And don't forget cloud gaming. If we connect with Xbox Cloud Gaming and the Meta Quest platform as our base, we're already ahead of half the developers out there." Shameer beams. "Pop pop's not just building a game. He's building a movement."

The two high-fives, more convinced than ever that the vision was bigger than just gameplay, it was about shaping the future.

***

At that same moment, Lee is in his den with Laura, preparing for something huge—his first investor pitch. His laptop is open, filled with mock-up decks, token tier graphics, and gameplay strategy slides. The family's ideas—VR, funding, platform integration—all fill the room like electricity.

Laura leans over and kisses his temple. "You're ready. They're going to love this."

Lee exhales deeply. "It's more than just a pitch. I'm carrying all of us into that room. You, the kids, my grandkids. This dream is ours now."

Laura smiles. "Then go speak from your heart. The vision has already been written. Now it's time to tell the world."

And with that, The Pitch is officially in motion.

The Baillum family, spread out in different corners of the house and city, are all part of something bigger than they even realize—every laugh, every brainstorm, every trade, every hug—it all fuels Lee's next step forward.

The World-Wide Swap and Trade / The Gift Challenge was no longer just one man's dream. It was a family legacy in the making.

That night, as the house finally grew quiet and the family drifted to their own corners of rest, Lee and Laura remained awake. Today's pitch was important, but tonight was about them—about love, legacy, and vision.

CHAPTER TWELVE
LOVE, VISION AND LEGACY

After dinner and family time, Lee and Laura retreated to the family room, glasses of her favorite '94 Du Bellay red wine in hand. Lee made sure Laura had everything she needed—her comfort, peace, and joy were always his top priorities. He adored her in every sense of the word.

As they curled up on the plush leather couch, the room glowing softly from the table lamp beside them, they began to reminisce.

"Do you remember how we met?" Laura asked, a playful smile on her face.

Lee chuckled. "How could I forget? That social network dating site changed my whole life." Their stories unfolded, side by side like pages of a cherished book. Lee has been solely focused on his work, never imagining love would find him again. He had been through his share of hardships, silent battles, disappointments, and years of just trying to survive. He was not looking for love... but when the time was right, it found him.

Laura's path had not been very different. After losing her first husband to illness and then her beloved father not long after, grief wrapped tightly around her. She stepped away from work and traveled to Kannapolis, North Carolina, to stay with her cousin Aaron. For four long months, she cried, prayed, and healed.

"I remember praying," Laura said, her voice soft. "'Lord, I come to you with a heavy heart... grant me the courage to face each day with hope and love...'" She looked at Lee, tears welling in her eyes. "That prayer carried me."

"You're the strongest woman I know," Lee said, squeezing her hand. "I'm grateful every day that God brought us together."

Laura nodded. "It's funny how two broken hearts became one strong bond. We took two families and made one. A blending of lives, built on love, faith, and real partnership."

Lee smiled. "We're more than lovers—we're teammates. You challenge my ideas, make me think deeper, and help me structure my vision. You take my dreams and shape them into something even greater."

"I do it because I believe in you," Laura replied. "Loving you comes easy. We've got that rare, genuine connection. You protect me, uplift me, and you've shown me a love that's patient, honest, forgiving—and most of all, real."

They clinked glasses and took a slow sip, letting the warmth settle over them like a blanket. Then Laura's eyes lit up.

"I see that look," Lee grinned. "What just popped into that beautiful mind of yours?"

"I have an idea," she said, leaning in with excitement. "You need to create a secure information screen for the game—a data system with protected and encrypted columns. Only certain fields should be editable; the rest should be locked. We need a separate screen for swapping and trading, for saved sets, saved lots, and saved states."

Lee nodded, fully engaged.

"Also," Laura continued, "every player needs to have equal advantages. No cheating. You will need multiple security layers—multi-factor authentication, antivirus protection, and routine backups. Even a pamphlet to educate users on staying safe while playing.

Lee pulled out his notebook, writing furiously. "That is brilliant, babe. This game will be huge. *The World-Wide Swap and Trade/The Gift Challenge*—a gift from our family and a challenge to the world."

Laura leaned in, her eyes glowing. "Can't you see it? Lights, billboards, headlines... 'One Man's Dream: Leandrew Baillum. Who is he?'"

Lee looked at her with deep admiration. "He's a man blessed by God, standing next to the woman who helped make his dream bigger than he ever imagined."

They embraced in silence, knowing that their love and their vision were not only changing their lives—but soon, the world's.

CHAPTER THIRTEEN
THE PITCH

It was early Saturday morning. A soft mist lingered outside, but inside the Baillum household, there was electricity in the air. Today is the day, Tudy said.

Lee was up early, pacing the kitchen floor in his favorite gray sweats and white T-shirt, holding a mug of hot coffee. He had rehearsed this moment in his mind a thousand times, but now that it was here—today, the day he would pitch *The World-Wide Swap and Trade/The Gift Challenge*—he felt every heartbeat like a drumbeat of destiny.

Laura entered the kitchen, calm and glowing in a long, cozy cardigan. She took one look at him and smiled.

"You're ready," she said, placing her hand over his heart.

"I hope they think so," Lee said. "I just want them to see what we see—what this game can become."

Laura nodded. "They will. Speak from your heart. You have the vision, the passion—and your family has your back."

By 10 a.m., the house was buzzing. The dining room had been converted into a full presentation suite: laptops open, sketches spread across the table, mock-ups, color charts, lists of rewards and user journeys printed and pinned to the wall. Lee and Laura had called on their trusted circle—family, a few local tech advisors, and a couple of interested community investors who had heard whispers about "that game project everyone's talking about."

RJ and LJ prepped the tech. DJ hooked up the sound system and a short trailer-style intro video he had produced the night before. Dee and BreBre handed out printed funding research packets and app suggestions. The kids quietly observed, eyes wide open, watching what it looked like when purpose met preparation.

Lee stood at the head of the table; Laura sat to his right. He took a breath and began.

***

"Good morning, everyone… and thank you for coming."

"My name is Leandrew Baillum. I am a truck driver by trade—but an innovator by faith. What started as a vision during long nights on the road turned into a dream, and that dream became a family mission.

Lee paused, eyes scanning the room.

***

"We call it *The World-Wide Swap and Trade/The Gift Challenge*—a global, interactive gaming platform rooted in gifting, trading, connection, and competition. But it is more than just a game. It is a bridge—between cities, between cultures, between generations."

He motioned toward the board behind him.

"This challenge is designed for families, individuals, gamers, creators, collectors—people looking to connect in fun, meaningful ways. Each player joins by uploading tokens, performing challenges, and swapping inventors across all fifty states. Every participant gets the same opportunity—five tokens per lot, of 1,000 trades. Incentives like cash, cars, vacations, bills paid—even homes are awarded through live events."

"And yes," Lee added, "this will be fully accessible: VR, mobile, console, PC, cloud gaming. With encrypted data, real-time gifting maps, multiplayer tracking, cross-play compatibility, and security education built into the platform.

He turned slightly and smiled at Laura. "All of this was built with love—and most of the foundation came from this woman right here."

Laura gave a proud nod as the room applauded. Then DJ hit play, and the trailer lit up the screen.

Music pulsed. Images of swapping, challenges, live maps, players in different states sharing and swapping inventory of tokens and messages—it was bold, inspiring, and powerful.

When the lights came back on, the room was silent—until one voice broke through. "This," one investor said, leaning forward, "is revolutionary."

RJ and LJ exchanged glances. Dee squeezed BreBre's hand under the table. Laura looked at Lee with eyes full of pride and possibility.

Lee closed the presentation with a final word.

"*The World-Wide Swap and Trade/The Gift Challenge* is not just about prizes. It is about purpose. It is about connection. It is about giving something of yourself to receive something greater in return. And with the right partners, we can take this dream from the Baillum home to homes around the world."

***

The Baillum household buzzed with a new kind of energy. The pitch had been a resounding success, and the family knew what came next: testing the game with the community. This phase was not just technical. It was personal. Every bug found, every suggestion offered, and every smile sparked during play would help shape *The World-Wide Swap and Trade / The Gift Challenge* into a legacy.

Lee, Laura, and Jelisa sat down to plan it all. Jelisa, with her international insights and psychology background, emphasized the importance of accessibility. "We need to make sure the game is simple enough for a 5-year-old but deep enough to keep a 99-year-old excited."

They designed the Community Beta Testing around one central idea: *inclusion.*

CHAPTER FOURTEEN
COMMUNITY BETA TESTING

Setting Up the Test Rooms

The first step was to invite families from different age groups, backgrounds, and tech levels to test the game. The Baillum set up six demo stations in the community center:

VR Station — Featuring Meta Quest and PSVR2

Console Station — Xbox and PlayStation

PC & Mac Station

Tablet & Mobile Station

Youth Corner — Guided test play for ages 5-12

Seniors' Circle — Assisted game walk-throughs for ages 60+. Each room featured:

Welcome signage explaining the game in plain language.

Step-by-step guides with visuals

Friendly volunteers from the Baillum family are walking players through

Monitors to capture real-time user activity and feedback.

***

What Is Beta Testing?

Lee explained it simply, using big pictures and easy words so everyone could understand:

"Beta testing means we are giving people the chance to play our game before it is fully finished. We want your help to see what works, what is confusing, what is exciting—and what needs to be better. You are now a part of history in the making!"

***

Getting Started: Welcome Orientation

Everyone gathered in the family room as Laura and DJ kicked off the welcome orientation:

Name tags were handed out by Shameer and Rodney

Everyone received a **starter kit folder** with:

A simple guidebook with pictures

A quick "How-To Play" cheat sheet

A feedback card

A mini token set

An avatar sticker sheet (for creating your player identity)

Kids got a **"Player Buddy"**—a teen or adult to guide them step by step.

DJ set up big screens showing the animated tutorial. The voice narration made the steps simple: "Step One: Choose your avatar—this is YOU in the game! Step Two: Pick your city and state is where your trading journey begins! Step Three: Use your five starting tokens to make swaps and collect gifts."

Every click was narrated and animated with bright colors, soft sounds, and fun music that kids danced to while the adults nodded in understanding.

***

The Game Zones

Lee created different game "zones" in the house and backyard, turning the home into an experience:

Trading Table – Where players could swap items using their tokens. Everyone had to

describe the value of what they were offering and why the trade was fair.

Gifting Garden – A quiet area where people could anonymously drop off or receive small gifts using tokens. A chalkboard asked questions like, *"How did this gift make you feel?"*

Tech Tent – Where players tried the game on tablets, desktops, and VR headsets.

Rodney and Shameer helped install and troubleshoot.

Storyboard Wall – Players could write down their game ideas and tell the family what they would add.

***

Keeping it Safe & Fair

Tudy explained to everyone:

"We want you to have fun but also be safe. So, we have helpers around who are called 'Game Guardians.' If something does not feel right or you are confused, tell a Guardian. Everyone plays fair here."

Passwords were simple and stored safely with help from the Game Guardians.

Swapping zones had rules posted clearly, using pictures for young children and descriptions for adults.

DJ, Jessica, Tudy and Dee walked around showing players how their information was protected using a safe, encrypted system.

Surprise: Prize Simulations

At 3 p.m., Lee called everyone together and surprised the crowd with *"Prize Simulations."*

"We want you to feel the excitement of winning. So today, some of you will be picked randomly to receive a simulated prize from the actual prize pool.

Winners received:

A free haircut or styling appointment at Bobby Daughter's Hair Line

Local amusement park passes.

Personalized gift baskets

"I Helped Build the Game!" T-shirts

Little Amorah, just 5 years old, squealed with joy when she received her basket filled with crayons, stickers, and a glittery token pouch. She shouted, "I'm going to play again, and again, and again!"

***

Feedback Time: What Did You Think?

After two hours of playing, Dee and Jelisa gathered everyone in the backyard. Each person had a chance to fill out their *feedback cards* or record a video on the DJ's camera.

Sample feedback prompts:

Was the game fun and easy to understand?

Did you feel connected to others while playing?

What part was your favorite?

What confused you?

Would you recommend this to your family?

What did you enjoy the most?

Was anything hard to understand?

What would you like to see added?

Kids drew pictures. Teens made TikTok. Adults filled out cards or spoke on camera.

***

Common Questions Answered

Q: "Can I trade with my cousin in another state?" **A:** Yes! That is how you grow your inventory. You can build Trade Screens to visit other cities and states anytime.

Q: "What if I forget to save my set?" **A:** Your coins are autosave, but always upload them to your Saved State Inventory Room for full credit.

Q: "What if I don't have internet?" **A:** The game has offline saved and local sync. Once you are connected again, your progress uploads.

Q: "Can younger kids play alone?" **A:** Children under thirteen require a guardian account, and there are built-in safety prompts to help them navigate.

Q: "What happens when I complete all 50 states?" **A:** You are officially entered in *The Gift Challenge*. The player with the largest verified inventory at year's end will be eligible for amazing prizes.

***

What They Learned

Back in the family room, Lee, Laura, and the rest of the Baillum crew reviewed the feedback. They saw:

Kids loved colorful avatars and wanted more dance moves.

Parents loved how the game promoted sharing and financial thinking.

Teens wanted more social features and faster swaps.

Seniors loved the gifting system and requested bigger text and voice-assist options. Brenda wrote down every comment. BreBre smiled and said:

"This feedback is gold. These people are now not just players… they are part of the creation of something that will go world-wide."

A Game for All Generations

CHAPTER FIFTEEN
CLOSING DAY

At the end of the final beta weekend, Jelisa gathered the family together.

"Today, we watched 5-year-olds and 75-year-olds play together. We saw smiles. We heard laughter. We got feedback. Now we fine-tune, polish, and prepare. Because this isn't just a game, it's the future."

Lee added with a hand over his heart, "And it's built by family, for the world."

The Gift Challenge had officially entered its final stretch before launch—powered by purpose, tested by the community, and united through love.

Children loved unlocking badges. Seniors appreciated the large font modes and voice instructions. Teens raved about the interactive trade boards. Parents liked the idea of a game that could be played together across generations.

That evening at Baillum's home, it was full of laughter, gratitude, and hope. Lee and Laura sat quietly on the porch, wine glasses in hand, watching the sunset.

"We're not just making a game," Laura whispered. "We're building a legacy."

CHAPTER SIXTEEN
LEGACY CONTINUES

The sun rose on a new chapter.

The Baillum household, once buzzing with planning, laughter, meetings, and beta testing, now hummed with quiet satisfaction. It had been a long, beautiful road—from idea to invention, from kitchen table notes to community-wide testing. And now, the World-Wide Swap and Trade / The Gift Challenge was real. Not just an idea or a dream, but a living, breathing platform built with heart, built with purpose.

Lee sat in his den, surrounded by empty coffee mugs, scribbled posts it notes, and printed game charts. On the screen in front of him: the first official email blast announcing the soft launch. "The Gift Challenge Is Here: Join the Global Movement." He stared at the line, smiled, and hit send.

Meanwhile, Laura was in the kitchen arranging a celebratory breakfast. Her phone buzzed every few seconds with texts, email alerts, and new online orders for the game. Jelisa was working on scheduling media interviews and community rollout events. She had already lined up a

TEDx-style talk for Lee at a youth innovation summit. The world was watching.

The entire family gathered around the dining table—this time not for brainstorming, but for reflection.

RJ and LJ took turns reminiscing about the first time Lee explained the idea to them—back when it was just a dream. DJ pulled out his headphones and shared a new music score he was composing for the live events. Shameer and Rodney passed around notes about the upcoming VR expansion and cross-platform analytics. BreBre, Dee, and Tudy gave updates on social media traction and ambassador partnerships forming in cities across the country.

Jelisa & Brenda stood at the head of the table, flipping through a leather-bound presentation journal. "We've accomplished something incredible. But this is not the end. It is just the prologue. The world is waking up to what we've built—and now, they want more."

Lee nodded. "They'll get it. The Gift Challenge is not just a game. It is a mindset. And the next phase... well, it's even bigger."

Amorah, sitting cross-legged on the floor with a glittery game token pouch, looked up and asked, "Does that mean we're going to keep building, Poppop?"

Lee leaned down and kissed her forehead. "Always."

ABOUT THE AUTHOR

Laura Baillum is more than an author; she is the heartbeat behind a vision that began as a whisper in the mind of her husband, Leandrew Baillum.

Laura is a devoted wife, loving mother, and unwavering believer in family. Laura has always known that when passion meets purpose, something powerful is born. For years, she watched the man she loved dream out loud—his ideas scribbled on napkins, spoken during long walks, and pondered late into the night.

One day, with a heart full of pride and a soul stirred by destiny, Laura picked up a pen and began to write. The result was *One Man's Dream: The World-Wide Swap and Trade / The Gift Challenge*—a tribute to the man she adores, the family she treasures, and the movement they've created together.

Laura writes not just with words, but with legacy. Her storytelling is rooted in love, uplifted by unity, and guided by faith. This is more than a book. It is the beginning of a new way to dream, to play, and to connect as a global family.

Because when one family dares to believe, the entire world gets permission to dream.

A FAMILY BUILT LIKE A MACHINE

Lee and Laura had always believed in the power of education, curiosity, and family. They never allowed shortcuts. They raised thinkers, builders, dreamers, and doers.

Family dinners were as sacred as paychecks. Laughter was medicine. Respect was non-negotiable. Love was the glue.

They didn't just raise children. They built a **legacy**. A unit that moved like a well-oiled machine—each part unique, but essential. Driven by faith, fueled by purpose, and rooted in the one truth that carried them through every season:

"Together, we build. Together, we rise."

One Man's Dream
The World-Wide Swap and Trade the Gift Challenge

"From One Dreamer to the World."

"When one family dares to believe, the whole world gets permission to dream."

Read the book

Play the game

Watch the movie

Join the movement

Become a part of the Legacy

One Man's Dream - The World-Wide Swap and Trade/The Gift Challenge

www.ingramcontent.com/pod-product-compliance
Lightning Source LLC
LaVergne TN
LVHW061221060426
835508LV00014B/1391